THE ILLUSTRATED
Cat's Life

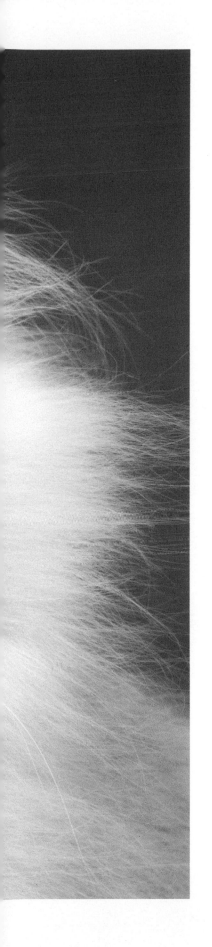

THE ILLUSTRATED
Cat's Life

Warren Eckstein and Fay Eckstein

GUINNESS PUBLISHING

Throughout this book cats are referred to as
'she' or 'he' in alternate chapters unless
their sex is apparent from the activity
discussed.

CONTENTS

INTRODUCTION

Your beloved domestic pet cat has a turbulent and exotic history, full of magic, religion, terror, and adoration. Perhaps it is because of their grace and beauty, independent natures, penetrating gaze, or strange cries. Whatever the reason, cats seem to inspire strong emotions in human beings.

THE SACRED CAT

Most cat lovers are aware that the cat held a special, sacred place in the hearts of Ancient Egyptians. Even their word for cat, *Mau*, proves by its sound how closely these people observed their feline companions. And most experts agree that the cat was first domesticated in Egypt.

However, there is some evidence to suggest that cats and man may have been sharing their homes for as long as eight thousand years. A feline jaw-bone was discovered in 1983 at a Neolithic settlement in southern Cyprus. Since Cyprus is an island with no wild cats, this animal must have been brought there specially.

Additionally, the bone proved to belong to the same species of cat later found in Egypt, a species with a larger head than the cats we know today. So it seems likely that the Egyptians simply took to extremes a practice already in existence.

One of the earliest paintings of a cat dates from 2600 BC, and was found in an Egyptian tomb of the Fifth Dynasty. This cat wears a collar, and, like all Egyptian cats, has tabby markings.

These cats led very comfortable lives. There are reports of Egyptians crumbling bread into bowls of milk for their pets, and carefully cutting up fresh fish for them to eat. They even tried to insure that females were mated with compatible males.

This passion for cats became a cult as time passed. There was a cat-headed goddess, Bast, who was linked with pleasure, fertility, music, and love. Cats appeared on magic amulets, bracelets, and were solemnly mummified when they died. In the nineteenth century archaeologists discovered more than 300,000 embalmed cats in a cemetery at Bubastis, site of the cat-cult's main temple.

Indeed, the Egyptians venerated cats so deeply that they shaved their eyebrows as a sign of mourning when one of their house cats died. If someone killed a cat, even accidentally, they were likely to be lynched by an angry crowd.

As this great civilization crumbled, the cat's special place inevitably diminished too. Some Romans, admittedly, worshipped the cat – and a domestic cat was preserved for posterity in the arms of a woman in the ruins of Pompeii. Certainly, by AD 79, cats were kept as a form of rodent control throughout the Roman Empire. During this period they became linked with the goddess Diana in her many guises as virgin huntress, fertility goddess, and goddess of the witches.

A PACT WITH THE DEVIL

Cats are nocturnal in their habits, their eyes glow in the dark, and their ability to move swiftly and silently can be unnerving. It was probably for such reasons that the harmless cat became inextricably bound up with witches, demons, and the dark powers of the unseen.

It was believed that cats had a pact with the Devil himself. They were thought to be able to cause storms, or to be witches in disguise. Terrible things happened to them; they were burned in ritual ceremonies designed to drive out evil spirits, buried alive, and cited in the notorious witch trials of the sixteenth and seventeenth centuries.

Hysteria and paranoia were at times so great that anyone who loved a pet cat might be suspected of dabbling in the black arts. The way cats enjoy sleeping upon their owners' beds, or curling up on their laps, was seen as evidence of some dark, demonic relationship.

These warped beliefs have survived into our own times. In 1929, for instance, there was a virtual epidemic of cat slaughter in Pennsylvania. It was

LEARNING TIME

By taking time to learn about the basic and finer points of cat behavior, body language, their care and, most of all, their need for love, owners can create a happier and healthier environment for their feline friends. But don't forget that it is equally important to know something about the psychological makeup of your cat. This can go a long way towards establishing a really strong owner/pet relationship.

believed that if a black cat was plunged alive into boiling water, and killed, one of her bones would make a powerful charm against witchcraft.

Even the hideous practice of burying a cat in the foundations of a building to bring luck has continued into this century. This ancient ritual was sometimes carried out with human sacrifice.

SYMBOL OF LUCK

Yet even through these dark times, some people continued to believe that cats were lucky. Buddhists believed that the presence of a dark cat would insure that a household never lacked gold. A pale cat would attract silver to the house.

In France, there was a belief in *matagots*, or magical cats. These wonderful felines would bring good fortune to their owners as long as they were loved and well looked after. Dick Whittington, who became Lord Mayor of London four times, had – according to legend – just such a companion.

Throughout history, some cats have found themselves in illustrious company. The Prophet Mohammed is said to have loved them; one story tells of how he cut off the sleeve of his robe because one of his favorites was sleeping there, and he was loath to disturb her. Popes and kings have also kept pet cats, while in more recent times President Theodore Roosevelt's cat, Slippers, was a regular guest at state occasions. Winston Churchill's ginger tom attended wartime cabinet meetings, while many artists and writers have kept cats as both companions and inspiration.

WATCH OUT!

Kittenhood is the most important stage of a cat's life. Personality, social patterns, temperament and individual characteristics develop at an incredibly young age. Although a cat's personal traits can be remolded and restructured at an older age, the best time to establish appropriate behavior and a loving disposition is during kittenhood and remember: kittens grow into cats very quickly. Be observant and it won't be too long before you understand what that bouncing bundle is saying.

ORIGINS OF BREEDS

It is generally agreed that the domestic cat originated from the breed *Felis sylvestris libyca*, the African wild cat. This species, which had faint stripy tabby markings, was the kind of cat found all over the ancient world. At some point it had been carried overseas by sailors, merchants and so on, and bred with other varieties of wild cat.

Regional variations also made their own contribution to the domestic cat we know today. One authority asserts that red or ginger cats originated from the Cape of Good Hope; reddish yellow from Central America; black and white with short tails from Japan; black from southern Russia; bluish gray from Europe and Siberia; black and beige from Thailand (formerly Siam); and tortoiseshell from Spain.

It was in the nineteenth century, in Europe, that cat breeding began in earnest. The first American cat show was part of a larger animal show held in 1884. In Britain one had been held in 1871.

If you visited a typical cat show today you would be dazzled by the sheer variety of cats on display. And expert breeders are still working hard to create yet more variation. But there are only seven main categories of pedigree cat, although around fifty separate breeds with numerous sub-classes and cross-breeds swell the numbers.

The longhaired breeds are divided into Persian, and non-Persian – known as Foreign Longhairs. Their bodies are low and thickset, with short legs. They have wide heads, broad noses and appealingly large, round eyes. These cats require a lot of grooming to keep their long silky coats looking beautiful, and to prevent tangling and matting.

The shorthaired breeds are divided into five categories. There are the American and British Shorthaired cats; Foreign Shorthairs; Foreign and Oriental Shorthairs; Burmese; and Siamese. Basically, American and British shorthairs have solid bodies with relatively short legs, rounded heads and ears, thick tails and are adaptable and robust. All "foreign" cats are more sinuous in shape, with tapering tails and an exceptionally lithe way of moving. They are also much more vocal than their Western counterparts, and often more active and inquisitive too. Their short, dense fur means that their grooming requirements are minimal, and although some breeds can be very demanding they do make wonderful companions.

ODDITIES

From time to time strange variations appear in litters of kittens. Sometimes these oddities have been deliberately mated to produce a breed. The Sphynx cat, for instance, has no fur and is sometimes recommended for allergic cat lovers. However, it needs a good deal of pampering, and cannot tolerate low temperatures.

Perhaps the oldest mutation is the Manx cat, which has no tail. These cats are a different shape from ordinary cats. Their back curves up toward the haunches, producing a strange, hopping style of movement. Sometimes a Manx will have kittens with tails, confirming that this breed is some kind of peculiar mutation.

Legend states variously that they were the last creatures to board the Ark, and Noah slammed the door on their tails by mistake; that they swam ashore from a shipwreck at the time of the Spanish Armada; and that Phoenician traders brought them from the East. Indeed, there is an almost tailless cat in Japan – the Japanese Bobtail. But research proves that the genes causing the Japanese cat's small, stumpy tail are not the same as those causing the typical Manx to have no tail at all.

The mystery remains unsolved. But then an air of mystery and glamor has always surrounded cats – and for the devoted cat lover, it will always be part of their enduring charm.

FACE TO FACE

It's a big world out there and most cats take to it quite nicely. Many even become brazen in attitude. Remarkably, the smallest of cats often find it no problem at all standing their ground against a large, even menacing, dog. When cats and dogs live together under one roof, it is not unusual to find that the cat rules the roost. Sometimes, the larger the dog, the more willing it is to relinquish its power and position to a tiny feline.

THE
KITTEN

EARLY DAYS

Caring cat owners should spay or neuter their non-pedigree cats, but if you do have a pedigree queen that you decide to breed from, you will be able to watch the miracle of feline pregnancy and birth for yourself. And for a cat lover there are few things more absorbing than seeing your own home--grown litter develop.

When she is having her litter the queen may want you around, or she may decide to be completely private. Respect her wishes, whatever they may be – and be prepared for quite a long wait. Thirty minutes is the average delay between the birth of each kitten.

Every kitten arrives in its own little membranous sac of amniotic fluid. The mother pulls this off, and immediately cleans the kitten's nose and mouth so that he can draw his first crucial breath. Then she bites through the umbilical cord and eats it. She will also eat the afterbirth, for it is full of nourishment. Finally, she gives the newborn a thorough wash and settles down to wait for the next arrival.

Each kitten is allocated a nipple to feed from. Amazingly, each nipple has its own special scent which the kitten recognizes and returns to: there is rarely any competition at feeding time.

RAPID DEVELOPMENT

Compared to human babies, kittens develop rapidly even though they are so fragile and helpless when first born. Their milky blue eyes will open in the first two weeks or so.

By the time the kittens are two or three weeks' old, they will be strong enough to move. At first they are delightfully unsteady on their tiny legs and they will not venture very far. But by three weeks they will be walking more purposefully, although they remain wobbly and tend to fall asleep where they stand.

A month or so after birth peace is at an end, for the tiny creatures have learned to run. Mom keeps a watchful eye on their antics, and scolds them if she thinks they are being over-confident. Give your litter lots of love and attention during these early weeks and the kittens will make much better pets, developing secure, loving personalities.

As they learn how to use their bodies, they are also learning how to play. Playing develops their hunting instincts, teaches them how to fight, and helps them create a relationship with you.

All this movement coincides with the early stages of weaning, which is not completed until they are eight or nine weeks' old. Kittens may take a few days to get used to eating solids, finding it easier to continue feeding from their mother. Encourage them to make the switch gradually. The mother cat will probably be rather skinny by now, and needs extra food, and vitamin supplements.

Once the kittens are on solid foods, they will need to learn how to use a litter tray. This process is usually very straightforward, for cats are fastidious creatures and the mother cat will encourage her young to use the tray. Make sure it is large enough and private enough for them – and keep it scrupulously clean or they will not use it. If a kitten looks as if he is about to urinate or worse on your carpet – he will crouch with raised tail – quickly place him in a clean litter tray. He will soon get the idea. Incidentally, always gently support a kitten's bottom with your hand when picking him up.

If he does have an accident, clean the area thoroughly or the lingering scent will persuade the kitten he can use the place again. Odor eliminator is available from pet stores.

CHOOSING A KITTEN

Choosing your kitten should be a happy experience for you both. In many instances the kitten, or kittens, will choose you. Sometimes in larger litters kittens seem to pair off. If possible, it is a good idea to take the pair. They will settle in more quickly, entertain one another, and ultimately give you more pleasure.

So, what particular things should you be looking for? Obviously, a lively, curious temperament is important. A healthy kitten is full of vitality, and quickly responds to a twitching string, drumming fingers or even shadow play. Do remember, however, that kittens need a great deal of sleep and if your visit is a short one you may not see them awake for long. Try to visit several times and also study the mother's character and behavior.

It goes without saying that your future pet should have a clean, shiny coat and bright eyes. Watery eyes and sneezing are signs of infection, as are a pot belly and generally undersized appearance. Unless you are prepared to spend time and money on the vet, it would be wise not to take a kitten in poor shape.

But, bearing these basic rules in mind, enjoy choosing your new companion. He will be an important part of your life for many years to come.

HIDDEN DANGERS

This little fellow has been allowed to wander in his owner's garden. But even such adventures are full of potential hazard. The list of plants harmful to kittens is lengthy and includes many of the popular spring bulbs as well as cottage-garden perennials and various shrubs. In fact, the experts recommend that kittens are kept indoors until a week after they have received their first vaccination against the commonest cat ailments, which is usually at nine weeks old.

Life as a tiny kitten can be a little cramped but the closeness offers a real sense of security to the defenseless newborn. The average litter numbers from three to five kittens and by squeezing tightly together they provide each other with warmth and the comfort of body contact. Potential cat owners should consider how many kittens were born to a litter (if the information is available). Cats born to large litters may present more aggressive behavior traits since as youngsters they may have had to compete with some of the other kittens for their mother's milk and for a space of their own. One little known fact is that it is possible that kittens from the same litter can actually have different fathers!

THE BABY

▶ *Newborns are hardly bouncing bundles of energy. Young infants greet the world not quite knowing which end is up. The first few days of life are spent quietly developing the energy and stamina which will be required for their new lives. Newborns are totally dependent upon their mothers for food, cleaning, and even for helping with their bathroom skills. Cats have a reputation of being able to fend for themselves. However, as far as newborns are concerned, nothing could be further from the truth.*

FIRST SIGHTS

Watching kittens develop is an unending joy. At birth kittens are very tiny, blind and deaf. By the second week of life they may have doubled their body weight.

This is also the time that their eyes pop open. Interestingly, all kittens are born with blue or blue/gray eyes. Permanent eye color doesn't develop until about

12 weeks of age. Facial expressions may also be seen for the first time and about now there may even be some general recognition of familiar people and

objects. But they're still babies and quite fragile. Plenty of tender loving care should be the primary concern.

NOW I'M GETTING THERE

Three-week old kittens begin to show the first real signs of growing up. Their ears, which were previously flattened against the head, begin to take on their adult prick-eared position and they have developed enough muscle strength to start exploring their environment. This little creature is clumsy and uncoordinated and is bound to take a tumble or two. Looking more than a little tight, he will, by persevering, rapidly learn to tackle the obstacles and challenges that are part of everyday life.

REAL FOOD

▲ Much to the relief of Mom, kittens enjoy their first taste of real food at about three to four weeks of age. Learning to lap up food and liquids doesn't always come easily and after mealtime kittens often need to have their mouths and chins dabbed off with a cloth. But the big mistake commonly made by owners at this stage is that they think the kittens' diet should be composed almost entirely of milk directly from the container. Quite the contrary. Milk doesn't agree with many small kittens and too much might contribute to tummy upsets. Kittens should be fed on a commercially made kitten diet.

T H E   B E S T   O F   P A L S

▼ *Young kittens need to bond with each other to develop healthy psychological attitudes. It's important for kittens to spend just the right amount of time with their littermates before they're separated. Kittens who are taken away too early are often denied the opportunity to interact with other animals. They may end up attaching themselves too closely to their new human owners and grow into submissive adults. On the other hand, kittens who live with their littermates for too long could grow up to be over-assertive, having played too many rough games with their brothers and sisters. Although experts vary on what the optimum age for separation is the minimum should be eight weeks of age and the absolute maximum 12 to 14 weeks of age. This should allow enough time for the kitten to socialize with the other cats in the litter while leaving enough young, impressionable time to adapt to a new life.*

LOOKING FOR LOVE

▶ *Kittens need all the love and kindness owners can supply. Go to extremes. The more loving, kissing, cuddling and gentle handling they receive at this age the more sweet and loving they'll be as adults. It's important to nurture them and to try to turn a blind eye when they've been naughty. Sure, they're bound to get into trouble at this age but harsh words or, worse still, harsh corrective treatment will only serve to create tough adult temperaments. Gently nudge them along the path to good behavior and try to be really patient. Shower kittens with love and affection and they will respond in kind.*

HAPPY LITTLE CAT NAPS

Who says cats don't smile? This little sleepy creature is clearly showing us that his world is perfect, at least for the moment. The contented little grin is easy to recognize and so is the "I'm so warm and happy" body language. By sprawling out on their backs when they are asleep cats demonstrate that they trust the people and the environment around them. It's a very vulnerable position, lending itself easily to attack by other animals. Most cats will only snooze like this when they feel all is right with their world. And then sometimes they will also smile.

ON MY OWN

▼ Help! I'm lost! You can almost feel how frightened this little baby is. Kittens get to a certain point in their lives when they think they're tough enough to run out on their own – that is until they turn around and find no one is behind them. The scared cry they emit while looking for mother is unique enough for her to come running to find and soothe her not yet so independent kitten.

NOW THIS IS MORE LIKE IT

▶ Although timid and frightened at first, it doesn't take a kitten long to get grass-roaming legs. Most cats develop a confident outdoor attitude. They must learn to be brazen yet appropriately cautious in order to survive outside. As kittens develop you can see the intensity and determination in their eyes. They'll quickly learn to stalk through their own personal jungles and adjust to the surprises awaiting them. And when something they don't want to tangle with appears they're clever enough to do an about face and skedaddle out of there. But, for the most part, they're brave and fearless and will at least tentatively test out new territory with a gingerly placed front paw to insure that the ground beneath their feet is firm and can be trusted to hold them.

SIMPLY ENTRANCED

▲ *At times kittens and even mature cats seem transfixed, almost mesmerized, as they repeatedly move each front paw up and down in almost rhythmic order. Called variously treading, kneading or trampling, this motion is actually a hold-over from earliest infant days when it helped to let the mother cat know that the youngsters were to be nursed. Kneading cued the mother's biological clock that it was time to produce milk. When an adult cat kneads on your lap or even your bed, it's simply an emotional throwback to the security of kittenhood. Although the claws may hurt, take the action as a compliment and resist any urge to correct the cat.*

BIG TROUBLE

◀ ▲ *Kittens and cats just love to play with yarn, string, rope or anything else that dangles. Too often owners encourage this and leave playthings around for a pet to play with even when he's unsupervised. Be aware that in an instant a playing cat could become hopelessly entangled in a long strand of fabric, or in the case of the swinging kittens pictured here, could be trapped and strangled within moments. It sounds grim but accidents like these are a reality, and they happen more than people realize each and every day of each and every year. Don't let a cat's fascination with yarn, hanging rope or the like bring him to an untimely death. He deserves better.*

I THINK I CAN!

If a kitten finally makes it up into a tree and then becomes too frightened to come down, try not to run to the rescue right away! Cat lovers may find it heartbreaking but it's best to allow little explorers to work things out on their own. Quietly stand by to be sure things don't get out of hand. If kittens can't solve the problem themselves, then human intervention will be required. But sometimes no action is the best action. After all, if a kitten doesn't learn how to climb down out of a tree this time, how will he know how to do it the next time he journeys in search of adventure to the boughs and branches above?

PRACTICE MAKES PERFECT

Oops! The world takes a bit of getting used to. It's a mistake to think that kittens instinctively have the know-how to do what seems so easy for their more mature counterparts. Cats' coordination skills develop slowly over a period of months. While it seems true that kittens can get themselves out of plenty of jams unscathed, don't believe that cats have nine lives. Caring cat owners need to keep an eye on young animals. Without interfering too much, try to be sure they're ready for the challenges they choose to undertake.

THE
CAT AT PLAY

One of the most enchanting things about cats is their natural playfulness. They are so sensual and responsive, and become so completely involved in their games, that they can distract and amuse all but the most stressed human beings.

Play can be a successful way to disperse tension in our lives. There are numerous historical examples of powerful figures who enjoyed playing with their cats. Cardinal Richelieu, for example, played with his 14 cats every morning before turning his attention to matters of state.

THE CREATIVE CAT

Cats are much more creative than dogs when it comes to inventing games for themselves, especially if there are two of them.

They also love to play with their human companions; some cats develop ways of signalling their desire to play with you. They may tap you gently on the leg or arm, or miaow in a special way which means, "Let's have a game." Oriental breeds are particularly vocal anyway, and are most likely to "ask" when they want to play with you.

Cats also seem to develop favorite games, and can become quite eccentric in their choice of toys. You may purchase special toys which your pet disdainfully ignores in favor of an old cork, pipe-cleaner, or piece of crumpled-up paper.

Both sound and texture are important to cats, and they usually prefer lightweight objects to play with. Cardboard rolls make excellent toys. Little sachets stuffed with catnip may send the most slothful cat into a state of ecstasy; catnip is to some cats (although others don't seem to have a catnip gene) what a couple of drinks might be to you.

FISH, MICE OR BIRDS?

Feline games are really mock hunting rituals, and can be roughly divided into catching mice or other small mammals; catching birds; and fishing. When you are playing with your pet it can be a good idea to bear this in mind, and play with them before meals. It may help your cat work up an appetite.

Mysteriously, some cats seem to concentrate more on one particular type of hunting play than any other. Mouse-type games involve chasing

something along the ground, stalking it and then pouncing upon it, using both front paws to trap the "mouse."

Cats who enjoy bird games love to leap up in the air towards a twitching string, or after a ball.

When cats or kittens toss something into the air, twisting around to pounce upon it, they are displaying their ability as fishermen. This interesting fact was discovered by some researchers observing cats fishing – something many felines do instinctively from a very young age. The tossing motion is exactly what they do when actually hunting fish – something you may see if you have a fish-pond.

In addition to these basic games, some cats will retrieve small objects and bring them back to you. This behavior seems to be particularly developed in Oriental breeds, or cats which have some Eastern blood somewhere in their make-up.

Curiously, the Ancient Egyptians took their cats hunting with them on the marshes of the Nile

delta. These cats acted as retrievers; perhaps the Egyptians simply took advantage of a natural instinct in this species, or perhaps those cats which retrieve today are repeating an ancient, learned behavior pattern.

DANGEROUS TOYS

Cat calendars invariably feature one picture of an adorable little kitten playing with a ball of wool or string. And although it is fine to wiggle a string along the floor for your cat, or dangle it tantalizingly in the air, it is unwise to allow your cat to play with string or wool by herself. This is because the animal could easily begin swallowing the thread and be unable to stop. Thread ingested in this way can cause strangulation of the windpipe unless veterinary help is sought swiftly. Similarly, although some cats seem fascinated by rubber bands, it is unwise to let your cat play with them – they may be swallowed inadvertently. These wrap themselves around the intestines, and again could actually kill your pet.

Other items to watch out for are balls of foil or cellophane, ping pong balls, corks, and small toys, any of which could be swallowed. Much as cats enjoy chasing a foil ball, or love the rustle of crumpled cellophane, you should never allow them to play with these items without supervision. Cellophane, if swallowed, can lacerate a cat's stomach. Foil can block up the intestine, and pieces of cork can choke her.

Commercial toys, too, should be viewed with a wary eye. It is really very similar to choosing a toy for a young baby. Is there anything which could be chewed or pulled off? Is there anything which might be swallowed? If the answer to these questions is yes, then it would be wise not to buy the toy.

As you and your cat, or cats, get to know one another you will develop your own games. Some patient owners have been able to encourage their cats to do little tricks, but the cat will invariably have invented the game. It is up to the owner to reinforce such behavior with rewards – such as lots of hugs, kisses and cuddles – so that the cat is motivated to repeat the game.

KIDS WILL BE KIDS

Cats can sometimes be like restless, little mischievous boys. When it's playtime, they tire quickly of the same old environment and often want to investigate something different. And like some kids they just love to play in the dirt or the next best grimiest place they can find. Exploring kittens and cats also love to hang out in their own private little hideaways, just like children who enjoy playing house or cowboys and indians complete with a make-believe house or fort. It's that escape to a private sanctum that's important. They feel secure and free to play in their own private world. But for curious cats woodpiles are the big winners. Stockpiles of wood or even a rotting tree trunk offer a challenge equivalent to mountain climbing as they wind themselves in and out and up and around. And such places are full of nooks and crannies which are perfect for a secret abode. Try not to be too harsh when kittens and cats come home dirty and unkempt – they've been having fun.

AN ALL-TIME CAT FAVORITE

You can spend a fortune buying kittens expensive toys and elaborate scratching posts and then find that their idea of a perfect toy is an old cardboard box or paper shopping bag. No matter, whatever makes them happy is fine. Here again, as with the cats and the woodpile, kittens enjoy the fantasies of their own little private world. If they seem emotionally attached to one box or bag, leave it around. But most cats enjoy exploring new ones. Hold on to all those boxes and paper bags (never dangerous plastic bags or bags with handles!) after each shopping trip and leave them about for the kittens to explore. Investigating the new "furniture" will help keep them mentally alert and make their daily lives more interesting. Next, try building them their own apartments by securing two large boxes together and cutting out cat doors between the "rooms". They'll love it.

ADORABLE BUT DANGEROUS

Popping up in the most curious places, kittens are sometimes so cute they could melt your heart. But within months those adorable little creatures reach the kitten equivalent of the "terrible two's." Even the most careful owner can be taken by surprise as their instinct for exploration develops quickly. This time this little one picked out a laundry basket to dive into and more than likely will be able to remove her head from the basket handle without injuring herself. But the next time she could crawl into the warmth of the clothes dryer or into a closet storing poisonous household cleansers. Inquisitive young animals need to be protected from themselves. Only allow kittens into environments that have been checked for dangerous articles. And don't take the adult cat for granted either!

CAT AEROBICS

It doesn't take much to occupy some feisty felines. A length of string and a dangling object create enough diversion for an afternoon aerobics workout. As any cat watcher can attest, cats have a real need to use their muscles. In the wild, nature provides physical challenges which ensure ample opportunities for cats to stretch their limbs. Indoors, however, the chance for extensive exercise can be limited, and pets may adopt sedentary lifestyle. Sometimes a very simple substitution will satisfy a cat's needs: a little eye-to-hand coordination (or should we say eye-to-paw) will delight a housebound animal but this toy presents hazards for the unsupervised cat and should not be left lying around.

CAT CONFIDENCE

Some cats are silly and just love to roll around at every opportunity, while others include rolling around in their play display. Sometimes rolling is a gesture of submission, and sometimes there's just no other way to relieve an itch. Often a roll on the back occurs after a lazy day in the sun or upon awakening from a nap. That's when a cat may greet a trusted human companion with belly uppermost. This very definite exhibition of cat body language means, "Hello, I'm glad to see you, but please excuse me for not giving you a more elaborate greeting right now." By exposing the stomach, which in felines as in many other animals is the most vulnerable part of the body, the cat is demonstrating confidence that the person being greeted will bring her no harm. Loving owners should not, however, be misled into thinking that all rolling cats will appreciate a belly rub. This may be a more personal and intimate greeting than a cat has in mind and could result in a cat biting or scratching the hand that does the stroking.

Is this little kitten playing with the grass or is she eating it? Given her position, it was probably the movement of this feathery specimen that initially attracted her. But it is not unusual to see cats munching long grasses and the habit has stimulated much speculation. Until recently the favorite explanation was that eating grass worked, sometimes as a laxative, sometimes as an emetic, to help cats eliminate hairballs trapped in the digestive system. However, experts now believe that eating grass provides cats with an essential vitamin called folic acid which is essential to healthy growth. Deficiency causes anemia because the chemical is needed in the creation of hemoglobin, the oxygen-bearing component in the blood. Owners of cats who never go out should plant a mini lawn in a seed tray. It's a simple solution which is as good for your house plants as your cat. More than a few cats and plants have come to grief in an urgent search for grass.

A QUICK SPRINT

▼ *It's not unusual for cats to make sudden mad dashes around their home or yard. This fleet-footed action has more to do with expending pent-up energy than anything else and should not be confused with chasing other animals for the kill. Sometimes this behavior worries owners of indoor cats: they're sure their cats are experiencing some form of seizure. But in almost every case it has more to do with spending too much time underexercised and insufficiently stimulated in an indoor environment. If this should happen to your cat, consider it her way of telling you that life is not as interesting as it should be. Be sure you do something about it.*

RATING INTELLIGENCE THROUGH PLAY

◄ *As cats develop they become more curious about the world around them. With that curiosity comes the need to paw and swat at their surroundings. Sometimes these actions can be aggressive but most often it is simply a sign of exploring, learning, or a play display. The more a cat uses her paws as an extension of the body, in the same way a human uses her hands, the more intelligent she may be. Although all this pawing and touching can certainly be frustrating for the owner of a cat who likes to investigate everything with her feet, take heart, you could be the owner of a budding cat genius.*

MISCHIEF MAKING

More than one clever kitten has used her paws as both fishing rod and reel. Others have learned how to open doors and have even been known to raid refrigerators. Owners of such coordinated cats need to stay one step ahead of their feline investigators. Cat owners should take nothing for granted. Safeguard your home before she figures out how to demolish it.

INVESTIGATING THE WORLD AROUND THEM

◄▲ *As disgusting as it may seem, some cats just love bugs. Interested kittens treat them like personal wind-up toys. Although some bugs move too quickly or slowly to be interesting, others seem perfect, either moving at a speed conducive to the chase or emitting a sound kittens just can't resist. Much to the horror of a queasy owner, a cat will sometimes go so far as to eat a bug. More often she'll play and paw at it like it's some part of a scientific experiment, and for her it is. She's curious – you can see it by her expression. Bugs are a part of her world and she wants to know all she can about them.*

40

THE
CAT IN A
MAN'S WORLD

Always remember that when you share your home with a cat you have taken him into your world. Cats may be amongst the most adaptable of creatures, but their natural curiosity can get them into serious trouble. So it is up to you not to take any unnecessary risks with their safety or sense of security.

DANGERS IN THE HOME

Statistics tell us that most accidents to people happen in their own homes. Home may be a refuge for both your family and your cats, but it is not always a safe place unless you take steps to make sure that this is so.

Simple actions such as loading the washing machine or tumble dryer, opening and closing the refrigerator, and any other closets or drawers in the house are likely to fascinate your cat. Cats are interested in everything, and because you are around they feel safe. If you are in a hurry, or thinking about something else, you may easily trap your pet somewhere for up to several hours without knowing it.

Numerous cats have got stuck in ovens, washing machines and other household appliances in this way. A full linen basket, for instance, may look like a cosy bed to the cat. If he burrows deep into the pile of washing, you may not see him until he is inside the machine – this is especially true of kittens.

So, obvious as it may seem, always look carefully when opening or closing anything in your home. This applies to windows too. Damaging falls or even death may occur if a cat gets out onto an upper ledge or balcony.

Needless to say, if you own a queen who is on heat the smallest aperture will suffice, for such is her determination to get out she will squeeze her body through apparently impossible gaps. You can either fit screens to your windows, or keep them shut unless you are in the room.

Around the house and yard, take the same precautions with your cat as you do if you have a small child. Household chemicals – including bleach, disinfectant, and some detergents – can be deadly. Keep these items safely locked up, or put away – or find safe alternatives, where possible.

Chemical hazards abound in the yard and the garage too. These include slug pellets, mice or rats that have died from poisoning, some brands of weedkiller, and paint stripper. There are also certain plants that are poisonous to cats. Even mature cats have been known to eat these, and kittens cannot be expected to know which are harmful. If your cat shows any sign of having been poisoned, get him to the veterinarian immediately.

IT REALLY IS A MAN'S WORLD

In a tangled maze of human possessions the cat finds his place. Cats have a great ability to adapt and this is the single most important factor they have going for them. As man's world changes cats change right along with it. From their days of living as revered pets of the ancient pharaohs right up to today, they have managed to stay with the times, never missing a beat.

CAT NAPPING

Cats love to lounge around and they always choose the best pieces of furniture for a snooze. Some studies indicate that they spend upwards of 70 percent of their time perfecting their sleep habits. But if a cat is spending more time than he normally does napping in warm places be sure to arrange for a check-up by a vet. There could be any number of medical reasons why his internal thermostat isn't working so his health should be assessed.

MOVING HOUSE

Moving house is stressful for both humans and animals, but with a little planning everything should go smoothly. While you are packing up it is sensible to involve your pet in the proceedings as much as possible. Have him out with the family, telling him what is going on. Put his food and litter tray in their normal places, and give him perhaps a cardboard box to play with and maybe some catnip (if your cat responds to it) to help him relax. As every cat owner knows, cats are sensitive creatures and they may become anxious in the midst of such preparations, for they dislike changes to their routines. Reassurance from you is needed.

When the time comes to leave, put your cat in his carrier and take him with you. On arrival at your new home, take him around and introduce him to his new surroundings. Find a quiet, private place to put his litter tray and his food, and give him food, water, and something to play with. This, along with extra hugs by way of reassurance, will help him to feel settled.

It is advisable to keep cats indoors for a few days after moving so that they can get accustomed to their new environment. Keep to their routine as closely as you can, and make sure they have their new address on their collars if they are going outside. Their natural curiosity should insure that they will enjoy exploring their new territory, and seeing off any intruders.

GOING AWAY

Going away on vacation or business need not be a problem for cat owners, but again it needs careful planning. Generally, it is far better to leave your cat at home and pay for a sitter or persuade a cat lover to come in and feed your pet. Cats are territorial creatures, and your home is full of familiar smells and sounds. These cushion the cat against the strain of being left alone. Keeping more than one cat is the ideal answer for a cat notices your absence far less if he has company.

If you can't get someone to cat sit for you, the options are to give your cat to a cat-loving friend to look after, or to put him in a commercially run boarding kennel. If you choose the latter, make sure you check out the kennel beforehand, and if possible go by personal recommendation.

On your return, give your cat plenty of attention and affection. Get down and spend time on his level, cuddling and hugging him. You will soon pick up your relationship where you left off.

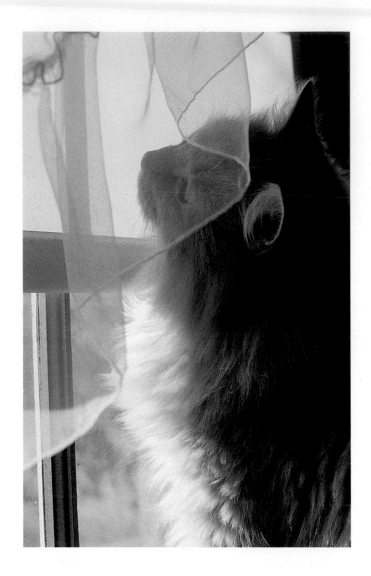

LATCHKEY CATS

Two-income households have created a new breed of cat – the cat who's left on his own, alone at home day in and day out. Some latchkey cats adjust well to being alone. They enjoy their free time and have no real objections to taking long snoozes. But others just can't cope with the loneliness. They stare out the windows, seemingly lost in space. Some become depressed and others get into mischief just to while away the hours. Some cats have been known to become downright destructive. All it takes sometimes to cure a suffering latchkey cat that gets along well with other animals is the addition of another cat into the household. They'll have each other's company to enjoy and the security of knowing someone else is at home with them all the time.

PLEASE DO NOT DISTURB

This cat has his own room – right beneath the stairs, complete with its own door for easy owner access. It's just personal space – some place special and private. Many cats enjoy a place of their own while others would rather be part of the family crowd, hanging out with the group, no matter what the commotion. By careful observation you can determine what your cat prefers. If privacy is his thing, be sure to set aside some space that belongs only to him. It doesn't have to be as elaborate as this, even a quiet cubbyhole in a seldom used room will do. Just treat it as his special place and, as you would do for any other family member, respect his need for a little space of his own.

 *It is truly amazing how many cats learn to sit up on the kitchen or dining-room chairs. Cats are clever and quickly learn that most of the interesting food in the house arrives on dining tables sooner or later. But this phenomenon of seating themselves at the table isn't only food related. Families come together at mealtimes and sometimes a cat just wants to be part of the social gathering. He may not be content merely to "stand by" at floor level and miss what's going on. Then there are all those cat owners who, when no guests are around and no one else is looking, actually encourage the family cat to be part of mealtime activities. Owners may not admit this in public but there are certainly a lot of them in the closet. These people would no sooner leave the cat out of a family meal than they would leave out a spouse or the kids. Sometimes the cat even comes first.*

CLEVER CATS

Cats may not have hands and fingers but they certainly make good use of what nature provided. Dexterity and agility are two great attributes of the average feline. Outdoor cats quickly learn to use their paws to push aside and then trample obstacles, and indoor cats acquire some very human skills. Some extraordinarily clever cats determine that twisting a door knob will open a closed door. Others have learned that even a refrigerator door is no obstacle if maneuvered correctly by agile paws. But almost all cats learn to use their paws for a dip and scoop. This action could be a throwback to feral days when water or a supply of fish had to be maneuvered out of a pond or stream or it just could prove that cats are ingenious. In any event, watch out for the milk and cream containers!

IS ANYONE WATCHING?

◄The game is on – sneaking up on the kitchen counter at every opportunity. Some owners don't mind while others have simply learned to look the other way, frustrated that their efforts to keep their cats off the counter have failed and resigned to living with a little bit of cat hair in all their recipes. Unfortunately, danger can await inquisitive, counter-jumping cats. Hot pans, sharp knives, scissors, meat bones or the like can all seriously jeopardize a cat's wellbeing every time he jumps up. Help solve the problem by lining the countertop edges with soda pop cans filled with small coins. When the cat jumps up, the cans fall down, making a startling noise as they hit the floor, and the cat receives his correction even if no one is at home to issue it.

THE BEST AND THE WORST

▲ ▶ *Cats are flexible creatures. They can blend into almost any environment and adapt to almost any set of circumstances. Throughout history there have been times when cats received royal treatment and times when cats have been scorned and left to fend for themselves. Today's cats experience both extremes, although many have a lifestyle somewhere between the two. Some are treated as best friends and live in pampered conditions, enjoying the luxuries and benefits of massage, their own beauticians, even their own jewelry. And, at the other end of the scale, some are treated as "disposable." Too many cats are abandoned when they are no longer wanted and forced to live on their own, eking out an existence on the streets – a sad commentary on how some people regard the world and how little respect is shown for life.*

EATING TO LIVE

Raiding the garbage is every cat's dream and every homeowner's and apartment dweller's nightmare. In no time at all the smallest of cats can wreak havoc and manage to strew garbage all over the place. When it's a well-cared-for neighborhood cat the resulting mess can be infuriating. But all too often the offending cat is a starving, unwanted stray, abandoned by its owners, or a byproduct of the overwhelming cat-population problem. Homeless strays reproduce at a mindboggling rate. Some conservative estimates indicate that one pregnant female and her offspring can produce over a million kittens in ten years. Each year millions of unwanted cats are either killed by humane societies or meet painful and untimely deaths on the streets. A cat's life isn't always what it's cracked up to be.

A REAL THREAT

Cats certainly can't outwit the automobile. Each and every day too many cats suffer a painful death under four wheels. Cats don't know to wait for the green light or look both ways before crossing. For that reason, and that reason alone, city and suburban cats should no longer be allowed outdoors to wander freely. In years gone by a cat lived his life in wide open spaces, free from traffic and congested conditions. But, today's cat is exposed to the threat of the truck, the automobile, the bicycle, and the bus. In many areas it is now simply not safe for most cats to roam. However, there is a solution: a cat leash and harness. This may not be what you want for your free-spirited cat but aiding and abetting a premature death under four wheels is not a responsible act for owners who claim to love their pets. In time a cat will adjust to a leash and harness, and the result will be a friendly animal who can enjoy the fresh air and experience the great outdoors and one who will live to tell the tale.

IT'S NOT ALWAYS FUN IN THE SUN

Although many cats are seemingly natural athletes, more than a few have no real experience in water sports so don't assume your cat can swim. Today's leisure time is often spent oceanside, lakeside, or even poolside. If water activities are on your itinerary, be sure your cat wears a life preserver. While they may be difficult to locate, they do exist and a responsible owner will scour the pet specialty shops and cataloges until one is found. Take no chances — the difference between life and death is often just a few seconds. And if there's a pool in the yard be sure there's absolutely no way a clever cat can find his way in. Better yet, be sure the cat learns to swim and knows how to climb out on his own should he wander in unsupervised. Accidents happen all the time. Teaching a cat to swim may sound like an impossible task but it can be done. The secret is to take it very, very slowly. Begin with just a few drops of water in a tub and when the cat is quite familiar and happy to play around in that, gradually increase the depth of water and so on, never pushing the pace beyond what your cat clearly enjoys.

THINGS AREN'T ALWAYS WHAT THEY SEEM

▲▶ The little black and white cat looks like almost any adorable feline getting into mischief and playing in the mud. But take a closer look . . . he's another one of God's forgotten creatures. Fending for himself, all this little one wants is a regular meal, any sort of roof over his head and a loving hand to stroke him and tell him he's wanted. There really is an excellent case to be made in support of spaying and neutering. It is the only way to solve the problems of unwanted cats and overpopulation. And it is one way to demonstrate we are the humane and educated society that we claim to be. Spaying and neutering won't make cats lazy and fat and it won't change their personalities for the worse. Indeed, many medical reports suggest that spaying and neutering may actually keep cats healthier and very possibly reduce the risk of their developing several forms of cancer. Spay and neuter those cats – it's the only sensible and caring thing to do!

DO FENCE ME IN

▶ *One solution to the problem of traffic hazards is the cat run. Fenced-in cat runs can be found all over the world, and not a moment too soon. Concerned owners and cat-care professionals use them because they recognize the cats' need for fresh air and sunlight in order to maintain good health. Homeowners have been known to build elaborate extensions on to their houses, while some practical apartment dwellers have built smaller extensions that attach directly to a window. A few clever manufacturers even market pre-fabricated outdoor cat rooms. Cat runs may become a necessity if the cat is to survive the technological disadvantages of coexisting with the human race.*

CURIOSITY FILLED THE CAT

◄ *Cats are intelligent and highly curious creatures, often interested in everything around them – not only the immediate environment. Balancing precariously in all sorts of positions (and even peeking through windows), cats will go to extremes to satisfy their inquiring minds, particularly if they feel excluded. The traditional feline reputation for being independent and aloof doesn't stand up for long when the candid camera is around.*

ON HIS OWN

◄ ▲ Tomcats on the streets have no choice but to fight for existence. Some are weak and don't last very long – the effects of scavenging food from alleyways and being ravaged by healthier, more dominant males simply takes its toll on these poor animals and they crawl away and die. The stronger, more cunning ones do live out longer lives – it's survival of the fillest in no uncertain terms.

Note the tattered ears of the tough-looking toms featured here. An ear is often the first thing injured in a cat fight. For this reason the fighting or aggressive cat often takes up a stance in which the ears are pulled back flat and swivelled against the head.

Cats will also instinctively pull back their ears when faced with a threatening situation. In that pulled-back position the risk of ear injury to an otherwise very accessible body part is greatly reduced. But classic body language or not, the ear is frequently the first area to be grabbed, chewed, and damaged in a cat fight.

THE
PHYSICAL CAT

61

Cats are blessed with highly developed senses designed to make them efficient hunters. But their responsiveness and sensuality also contribute greatly to our enjoyment of cats as pets.

SIGHT

All cats have highly developed vision, for it plays a crucial role when they are hunting and helps them to locate moving prey at some distance. Each eye has an angle of view which is more than 200 degrees, and the fields of vision overlap. With their mobile heads cats are therefore able to view a wider sweep of terrain than a human being is capable of seeing at one glance.

Rapid pupil dilation and contraction also heighten their visual skills, helping them swiftly adjust to changing light conditions. Their beautiful eyes can change in an instant.

Experts are now certain that cats do see in color, but not as intensely as we do. Feline eyes are designed primarily to react to light intensity. They contain a layer of reflecting cells which enable them to see light when human beings can perceive only the deepest darkness. It is this extraordinary ability to reflect light which makes cats' eyes appear to glow in the dark.

SMELL

Cats adore smells, and are fascinated by them. Catnip, valerian, perfume, cooking smells, their human family and other cats, all provide a rich source of experience and information. They make full use of their sense of smell to locate food, love, attention, and sex. An unneutered female cat in season emits a special smell which helps attract possible mates from the surrounding area.

A cat's sense of smell is so much a part of her personality that she may lose interest in food if she is suffering from nasal congestion.

TASTE

Cats have taste buds situated all over their tongues, and especially concentrated on the tip, and at the back of the mouth. It is rare for cats to have a sweet tooth; they respond above all to meat and fish flavors.

Cats also have a special sac on the roof of the mouth for "taste-smelling." This transmits information to the brain. The cat traps airborne molecules on her taste buds and flicks her tongue onto this sac. Tom cats use the technique to locate the sexual scent of females in heat, and it is also used by cats to gather territorial information.

PERSONAL PEDICURES

Some people think nail biting is a sign of a nervous cat and this certainly could be true if the animal lives in a neurotic household. But, she could simply be taking care of her own pedicure. The lifestyle of the average urban cat today offers too few scratching opportunities for this essentially outdoor animal so more than a few cats will bite their claws to keep them at the right length. It's not as strange as it sounds. When the claws get too long, they actually interfere with how cats distribute their weight while standing. Long claws throw cats off balance and may even aggravate an arthritic condition. To maintain a healthy cat, owners should be careful about keeping up with claw-trimming procedures.

HEARING

Feline hearing is very acute; cats can pick up sounds even dogs cannot hear. Their ears are wonderfully designed, with a set of muscles at the base of the earflap which can rotate the ear 180 degrees to pinpoint exactly where a sound is coming from.

Inside the ears are ridges which collect and concentrate sound. Such extra-sensitive hearing enables your cat to distinguish your step (or the sound of your automobile) from what seems like a supernatural distance.

When your cat is really listening to you, her ears will be pricked forward. Most cats are aware of their owner's voice, but often choose to ignore it unless it is saying something they want to hear.

Some cats appear to like music, while others seem indifferent. Observers claim that certain notes trigger particular reactions, notably, protective parental or sexual feelings, and simple self-protective behavior. Virtually all cats dislike very high-pitched notes because they sound like another cat in distress.

TOUCH

Cats are covered in touch spots – properly called tylotrich pads. Their function is to send yet more signals to the nervous system. Their paws and nose pads are especially sensitive. Delicate receptors in the tip of the nose help cats to differentiate between heat and cold.

Whiskers are also vital organs of touch. They can be moved closer to the head, or spread out in front to provide sensory information about nearby objects. They respond to changes of air pressure and to movement, and some experts suggest they could be part of a cat's early-warning system when it comes to detecting the approach of a big storm. Never allow a child to pull a cat's whiskers for they are exceptionally sensitive. "Guard hairs" on the coat also contain touch receptors which can tell cats how near they are to objects which are out of their field of vision.

A SIXTH SENSE?

Arguments rage, and have done for centuries, about the existence of a "sixth sense" in animals. Cats possess such heightened natural senses that they can absorb more information about the world about them than we can. But there are times when they seem to see something that we cannot. Happily for those who love the unknown, the scientific reason for this remains a mystery.

CLEANING UP

We rarely stop to watch how cats accomplish their personal hygiene. If the area a cat wishes to clean can be reached with her mouth, she'll simply take the easy way out and wash it directly with her tongue. But for those body parts she can't reach with her mouth she'll use her paw as a "built-in" washcloth. She thoroughly washes her paw, then rubs it on the appropriate body part. An agile paw can get to all those hard-to-reach places.

MOTHER-TO-BE

Pregnancy is no easy condition for most animals and it will certainly be no different for this mother-to-be. In the case of cats, the act of mating is arduous as well, at least for the female. After a very brief mating, usually lasting only seconds, the female will often cry out in pain and usually swats at the fleeing male. But, as nasty as it may seem to us, she is generally interested in repeating the process. Once pregnant, she will gain a few pounds, swell around the belly and in approximately 59 to 68 days produce her adorable litter of kittens.

THE DEMANDING KITTEN

In the world of mammals nursing has a special significance for infants and mothers and this certainly holds true for the feline family. It's a time of closeness and bonding. Amazingly, kittens seem to know instinctively that by kneading or trampling at the mother's belly, milk will miraculously appear. And it is a miracle of sorts because it is the kitten's kneading, moving the paws up and down in rhythmic order, that cues the mother it's time to feed the babies.

THE TIES THAT BIND

◄ ▲ *It's best not to interfere with a watchful mother. You can tell these mothers know their job and you had better not think about disrupting the comfort of their young. Young kittens also seem to know that the only safe time to rest is when they're snuggled up close to mother or the rest of the litter. This is an important time for mother and kitten to establish the ties that bind. What mothers want is a place that's secure and comfortable. A fruit box full of cedarwood chippings or crumpled newspaper in an undisturbed place will do just fine.*

▲ Mother cats have to move their babies somehow, the only way they usually can, picking up the kittens by the scruffs of their necks. They will try to keep their heads as high as possible to avoid dragging the kittens across the ground. The kittens curl up to make the job easier. Generally, mother cats carry their young during a "nest-moving" exercise. They choose to change nurseries for various reasons. They may feel the nest area is soiled or too small for the fast-growing kittens or they may sense that there are unfriendly animals around. They may simply be seeking out a quieter location for their families.

A FAMILY CUDDLE

▶ Mothers are very tolerant. Although this cat must be uncomfortable with her offspring squeezed around her throat you'd never know it by the look on her face. Actually, there are some studies which indicate more is going on here than just a family cuddling and snoozing together. It's possible that this close facial contact is an important way for a mother cat and her litter to get to know each other. Cats have important scent glands near their mouths and these kittens may be positioning themselves to smell each other better, so establishing a stronger bond.

A FOSTER MOM

Although there's no way of knowing from this snapshot, the photographer tells us that this adult cat is not the mother of these kittens. She's an aunt who lost her own litter. Many lactating cats will play foster mother to abandoned kittens or to young ones who have lost their own mothers. But why will a cat allow a strange offspring into her own brood, particularly when she's so protective about their care? Although we may never know for sure, one interesting and plausible theory suggests that the biological make-up of a very young kitten differs from that of an older cat and throws off a distinct odor which an adult cat can detect. It could be that the scent tells the foster mother that this is a defenseless baby in need of help, love and attention.

THE CANINE SURROGATE

The same theory – of a particular juvenile odor which lets an adult cat know that an orphan kitten is harmless and in need of nurturing – may hold true for a canine surrogate mother. Without a blink of disapproval this English bull terrier has allowed a feline infant to enjoy the comfort and companionship of her litter of puppies.

Owners apprehensive about introducing a second pet into households where there is already a cat who is not fond of other animals may want to keep this point in mind. Sometimes adult cats will sense the young, defenseless nature of puppies or kittens and accept them into their homes. Clearly great caution should be exerted to

insure neither pet is injured should the adult take a dislike to the newcomer. But often a pet that will not tolerate being around another adult animal will change its ways around a juvenile. Frequently, in such cases, they continue to build on their relationship so even when the whippersnapper grows up the two stay buddies.

LEARNING HOW
TO LAP

▼ *Kittens learn to lap up liquids at a very young age. At first they may not quite have the hang of it and stick too much of their faces into their dishes. . .*

▲ *. . . but in no time most cats get it right – keeping their heads at an appropriate height above the dish and letting their tongues do the work. Flicking in and out of the mouth and curled at the end and the sides, the tongue acts like a spoon, transferring liquid from dish to mouth.*

MMM-GOOD!

After a meal or a drink it's not unusual to see cats lick their lips and wash off the fur surrounding their mouths. Contrary to what most owners believe, lip licking isn't restricted to cleaning activities. Sometimes it indicates that a cat is a little nervous or distracted by something going on around her. However, it is important that owners should always be on the lookout for abnormal amounts of licking around the mouth. Many cats suffering from some form of dental pain will spend more time licking or pawing around their faces and jaws. Some studies suggest that over 90 percent of all cats have some form of tooth or gum disease by the age of five. So observe your cat carefully. She may be telling you she needs a dentist!

CAT MAKEOVERS

◄▲ *Grooming may take place for a variety of reasons besides the obvious one of keeping the body clean. Although we may never know for sure why cats spend so much time on the activity, there are several theories. These include the notion that licking and grooming* smooth out the coat and help it act as a better insulator against cold and heat; that Vitamin D from direct sunlight may be licked from the coat and ingested into the cat's system; and that it's simply a nervous reaction, similar to a person chewing gum, smoking a cigarette or biting the fingernails. But whatever the reason, forget the old wives' tale that cats can best take care of their own grooming needs. The more help they receive from humans the better: the less likely they are to gag up hairballs. And have you given any thought lately to bathing your resident cat?

Cats need to be bathed! Just ask any professional show-cat breeder or cat judge. However, if your cat has never received an ''official'' bath, introduce her gradually to the sink and bathing paraphernalia. She may not immediately take to a bath like the proverbial duck to water.

FLUFFY HITS THE TUB

Everyone knows cats are fastidiously clean. On any given day they spend a fair amount of time tending to their personal grooming. But, contrary to popularly held opinions, grooming does not come easily or instinctively to kittens. This little creature is making one of her first attempts at good hygiene.

Until recently the mother cat has been providing most of the necessary cleaning but now it's time for this kitten to start being responsible for her own needs. Although she's getting the idea, her uncoordinated position tells us she's a novice and hasn't yet perfected the finer points of bathing.

An adult cat, on the other hand, demonstrates impeccable grooming technique. This photograph is particularly interesting because it captures the cat in a classic position. It is a perfect study in body language.

DO CATS DREAM?

◀ ▲ *This is still one of the great unanswered questions. Most owners have long had sneaking suspicions about feline sleeptime imagery as they watch paws that twitch, legs that run and whiskers which flutter wildly. But scientists are only now confirming that the odds that cats do really dream are indeed quite good. Some recent studies seem to indicate that cats enter into REM (rapid eye movement) sleep, the type of sleep during which, in humans, dreams generally take place.*

SLEEPING WITH ONE EYE OPEN

▲ Snoozing in the sun is a favorite pastime of many cats. Although this cat's stretched, relaxed body indicates she's certainly enjoying the springtime warmth, she hasn't yet committed herself to a complete loss of control by closing her eyes. Very often when cats partake of their little cat naps they don't fully trust their environment. They may seem to be nodding off but you'll find that they are keeping an eye on what's going on around them.

YAWN, STRETCH... NOW I'M AWAKE!

After a cat nap or a full evening's sleep it's not unusual to see cats stretch and yawn. Like people, they take time to wake up. Also, just like people, cats may not be in the best of moods or can be easily startled while still groggy from a nap. Humans run the risk of being bitten or scratched if they brazenly intrude into their world when they are languishing somewhere between sleep and waking. So allow a cat some quiet time until she is fully alert. This is an important point to remember, particularly if you have children. Teach kids to respect the rights of their feline playmates.

I'M SCARED!

▲▶ The way cats choose to move tells us a lot about what's taking place in their minds. These cats have both been frightened: their stance tells us all we need to know. The way they arch their backs shows us they are alarmed and their bristled fur lets us know they are unsure of the situation around them. Both of these actions help to make the cat appear as large as possible in the eyes of an aggressor. In addition, the kitten's paws are poised ready for immediate flight in almost any direction she chooses.

FATHER KNOWS BEST

Sometimes father knows best; at other times the mother cat sets the tone for teaching the difference between right and wrong. In any event, whether or not the cats are related, an older cat frequently will act instinctively as mentor or instructor for a young whippersnapper. Mature cats generally get a point across by issuing a gentle smack or a menacing growl. Unless there is a serious bout involving bloodshed, when a kitten is being rebuked humans should take a back seat and not interfere. If there's more than one feline in your household, one cat needs to be in charge, and it's best for everyone concerned if the older, more experienced cat is calling the shots. Most homes could do without a delinquent kitten making the decisions.

PATIENT PARENT

A good feline parent, just like a good human mom or dad, will sit by, ever patiently, and watch the little monster, pretending to be interested in those adolescent games – no matter how silly or boring they may be. It's part of being a parent!

In an outdoor world suburban and rural cats have more outlets for scratching than they know what to do with. A wooden post here, a tree trunk there, virtually around every corner there's a suitable item for scratching and clawing to help keep claws at the proper length. City cats who are kept indoors don't have this naturally occurring scratching paraphernalia. Owners of indoor cats usually substitute a commercially made scratching post. If they're very lucky, one post will suffice but for active cats a single one simply doesn't offer enough variety. Not only will the post get scratched, so will the couch and the wood paneling. The solution is to buy or build a number of scratching posts, or bring in insect- and pesticide-free logs from outdoors. The cat will love them and you might just rescue the furniture.

◄ *Many animals claim their territory by some form of "marking" behavior, and cats are no exception. All cats do it, although it is more frequent and has more obvious effects when unneutered males "spray" fence-posts, walls, and so on with urine and anal-gland secretion. Marking outdoors is generally tolerable, but if a cat is confused and marks indoors, owners have to endure hours of scrubbing and cleaning to relieve their homes of the obnoxious smell. For cats with a discretion problem keep the litter box extra fresh and clean to encourage more use. Also, try feeding the cat in his favorite marking spots. Cats are usually reluctant to soil and mark an area where their meals originate.*

THIS IS MY SPACE

In much the same way as cats "mark" to let other animals know they are in the neighborhood, cats of both sexes will rub their mouths on different items. The mouth has certain scent glands and cats can leave their scent by rubbing their mouths up and down against tree branches, furniture and even people, so claiming them as their own. However, there can be even more basic reasons for rubbing – perhaps the cat just has a dirty or itchy mouth and no other way to clean or scratch it. Although cats are complicated creatures, don't make the mistake of overlooking the obvious.

A TASTE FOR PLANTS

Everyone knows to take time to smell the roses, but why do felines nibble the begonias? This habit of plant eating may not be as strange as it seems. Some experts believe a cat's sense of smell is four to five times better than that of man, so the garden provides a perfumery of interesting smells. Cats also instinctively lick some plants for vegetable extracts. Cat owners with plants need to beware. Lily of the valley, dieffenbachia, foxglove, and American, English, Japanese and western yew are among the hundreds of plants and flowers which are poisonous to cats. Some can be fatal so it's important to check with your local plant nursery expert for safe plants to grow, such as catnip or grasses.

STANDING TALL

Although cats are four-legged creatures, it's not unusual for them to adapt to a two-legged stance. Some cats can accomplish this by either standing up against or leaning on a solid or stationary item. Others can stand tall without any assistance. However, the question remains: if cats have such great agility on four legs just why do they try to improve their abilities by negotiating life on two legs? Simple. It's a big world out there and cats are quite tiny. In order to get a clearer perspective on the rest of the world they have no choice but to reach upward on their tippy toes to see what life has in store.

COOL CATS

▲ It's a hot day – you can tell by the greenery and the light coming through the bushes. This smart cat has opted for the shade of the underbrush to escape the heat. She's black and so all the more sensitive to the hot rays of the sun. Regardless of color, any cat can fall victim to heat stroke. Cats do perspire but not to the same degree as humans. They don't have sweat glands or pores distributed all over their bodies but sweat only through the pads on their feet. Also, nature has thoughtfully provided them with their own personal air-conditioning systems – panting. Through panting cats can reduce their body temperature. So, when the outside thermometer rises, be sure your cat has shade and plenty of cool, fresh water or she could fall victim to the effects of heat. Be alert for the early signs of stress – excessive panting and deeper pink or red tones of the inner ear, tongue and gums. Be extra careful with older cats, young kittens and those breeds with "pushed-in" faces like Himalayans. They're all a good deal more sensitive to the effects of the heat and direct sun.

THE CATNIP GENE?

◄▲ Catnip is a little plant that packs a big punch. When exposed to catnip, some cats have wildly hallucinatory experiences, complete with rolling, bursts of running and, at times, even aggressive behavior. Other cats have milder reactions, and some cats have no reaction at all. Why should catnip have such wildly differing affects? The most recent theory is that it's genetic.

Some cats have a "catnip gene" and some cats don't. Those possessing this gene react to catnip in varying degrees. Controversy rages over whether or not cats who react to catnip should be exposed to what appears to be the equivalent of a mild drug. If you're facing this dilemma with your cat, the consensus seems to be that a little catnip every now and then is probably alright.

THE CAT AS PREDATOR

Many of the things you love about your cat – grace, balance, and playfulness – spring from his skills as a hunter. For even the most pampered pussycat has all the instincts of a mean hunting machine.

LEARNING TO HUNT

Already, when they are only three or four weeks' old, those adorable kittens are busy developing hunting skills. But they will not acquire the full range of techniques unless they remain with their mother until about three months' old.

The mother, or queen, instructs her litter in the finer points of hunting and killing. These teaching sessions may well offend a squeamish owner, for she brings back live prey to demonstrate what should be done.

Should your cat bring you a small bird or mouse which is still alive, you may assume that he is attempting to encourage you to learn how to hunt. This is why spayed females seem to bring prey for their owners more often than other cats. Deprived of a litter to teach, the human owner temporarily becomes a kitten as the female acts out her frustrated mothering instincts.

PLAYING WITH PREY

Cats' habit of "playing" with their prey seems very cruel to us. But in truth cats are not sadists. Apart from the actions of the mother cat instructing her litter, there are two other reasons why cats appear to torment their half-dead victims.

Domestic cats generally don't need to supplement their diet by hunting. But this instinct is so powerful, and brings so much pleasure, that it cannot be suppressed for long. Some experts maintain that pet cats therefore try to spin out the catching and killing process.

Another reason for this behavior is obviously self-protection. Rats are dangerous creatures capable of inflicting deadly bites. So, before even attempting to kill it, cats will try to stun their victims with rapid blows from their front paws.

HUNTING MOVEMENTS

Pouncing, stalking, leaping, and swiping are all familiar movements to cat lovers everywhere. But there are other, less obvious movements which may puzzle you when playing with your cat – or watching his attempts to catch a bird.

SOUNDING MEAN

Most people associate growling with dogs and never expect an adorable feline to issue such a menacing sound. No matter how sweet and adorable they may be, some cats do growl, while others only hiss and spit. Regardless of what noise a cat utters his reasons for doing so remain the same. When ready to attack or when feeling threatened, a cat needs to appear as tough as possible. Aggressive noises add to the image. No one wants to challenge something that looks and sounds so mean and threatening. There is a well-respected theory that cats learned to hiss and spit by mimicking snakes, but it seems more likely that cats are sufficiently clever to devise their own warning and aggression signals without doing snake imitations.

Cats learn to stalk prey partly from instinct, and partly from their mothers. The sounds and motions of small animals seem to trigger an automatic alarm clock. This cat is demonstrating the classic technique of the hunt. Here he makes full use of the high grass around him in a slow, cautious crouching movement which allows him to camouflage some of his body.

Sometimes you may see your cat swaying his head rhythmically from side to side. This strange movement is actually helping the cat to estimate the distance between himself and his victim – or even the piece of string you are playing with.

Another curious movement you may observe is tail wagging. This rapid movement signals conflict, and occurs when the animal is hunting something but has not found any suitable cover. Pulsing with adrenalin and the desire to attack, instinct nevertheless tells the cat that he is getting all worked up for nothing, because his victim will probably spot him and escape. Conflict results, and the adrenalin finds an outlet in tail swishing.

But cats are patient creatures. Their ability to concentrate, bide their time, and wait for exactly the right moment stands them in good stead when hunting. Their acute sense of hearing is another important asset when hunting. This tends to decline from the age of three or four, and may gradually affect their skill as a hunter. Deaf cats are unable to tune in to the high-frequency noises emitted by typical prey, such as rodents or birds.

HISTORICAL HUNTERS

Cats have been valued for their hunting abilities for thousands of years, and since the days of the Ancient Egyptians they have been used to protect grain stores. In tenth-century Wales cats were considered an important part of the household. When a Celtic marriage was dissolved, the law stated that the couple's first cat went to the husband, whereas the wife claimed the rest.

Strangely enough, this recognition of cats' value as natural rodent controllers was lost during the time of the plagues in the seventeenth century. Many cats were destroyed because it was wrongly believed that they carried the deadly infection.

Japanese high society also misunderstood the relationship between cats and their prey. Cats had become very fashionable in medieval Japan, thanks to Emperor Ichi-Jo, who had imported a white cat from China. Pampering pet cats outrageously soon became the ultimate in Japanese chic. They were often kept, rather unkindly, tethered by silken leads. Believing that hunting was an undignified activity for their beloved pets, the Japanese decided that images of cats should be enough to deter rats and mice.

Numerous beautiful paintings of cats were placed in prominent positions to protect grain crops and precious silkworms. Of course, this solution was doomed to failure. Eventually a law was passed stating that all cats should be freed to do what comes naturally. Today, the cat remains a potent good luck symbol in Japan.

TAKING IT SLOW

◄▲ While stalking, cats will frequently pause a moment to get a better fix on their prey. Often there will be a series of pauses before the final ambush. Cats prefer to pause in areas which give them some cover or camouflage but sometimes that's just not possible. Many a suburban cat has only short, well-manicured lawns to hide in while the cat pictured left has nothing but a layer of snow. This one is undeterred. He crouches down as low to the ground as possible while watching every movement of his soon-to-be victim. Depending on the distance that needs to be covered, the cat may repeat the crouch, run, crouch sequence several times before pouncing on his unsuspecting prey. In one swift and seemingly effortless motion he rises from behind his cover, exposing himself to the prey, and pounces so quickly that only the most alert animal is able to escape his clutches. The intensity of the hunt is apparent on the face of the cat above. You can sense the readiness in his body. Every muscle seems primed for the pounce.

RESCUING FEATHERED FRIENDS

Not all cats are interested in catching birds. It seems to be a trait they're either born with or develop from watching other cats around them. If a cat is a die-hard bird chaser, then oftentimes there's just no stopping him. These feline hooligans demonstrate that they'll go to any lengths to satisfy their murderous appetite. Bird killing poses a tough dilemma for many cat owners. It is heartbreaking to witness the slaughter of beautiful backyard birds. Attaching a bell to the cat's collar is usually the best solution although it's not always effective. Seek out a small, lightweight bell which is sufficiently noisy to warn off the birds and attach it to a pop-away collar. Should the cat's collar become entangled with the underbrush or caught on the branch of a tree, this type will allow

him to pull free without
injuring his neck or
becoming trapped. Of
course collars with bells are
annoying to cats but many
owners feel very strong that
they are just one more item
a modern cat must put up
with for peaceful
coexistence.

Horse barns and cats seem to go hand in hand. In almost any part of the world where there's a barn there's bound to be a cat, or two, or a couple of dozen. People who love horses seem to have an affinity with most of God's smaller creatures and enjoy the opportunity of providing room and board for a few extra feline pals. Tack rooms are an especially favorite spot for cats. On the one hand they are out of the way of the general hubbub but on the other hand there's usually someone around to rub against or to dole out a quick pat on the head.

OF MICE AND MEN

As with bird catching, some cats are good mousers and others don't seem to care much for the activity. Throughout history a large percentage of them have demonstrated their interest in the rodent hunt. During certain periods when cats were disliked and even actively destroyed, it was only their expertise in keeping down the rodent population that brought them back into favor.

Cats will often present you with their kill or leave the corpses on the doorstep as if they were a welcome surprise. Although it's hard to stomach finding a dead bird left as a gift, most owners find a rodent more vile still. In any event, as upset as you might be, try not to scold the cat. Simply dispose of the catch as discreetly as you can. Remember the cat is behaving according to his nature. You may not want to encourage this behavior but criticizing it could create neurosis.

DOWN ON THE FARM

On the more practical side of things barn cats serve a real purpose. The animal feed that is inevitably stored there is an open invitation to rodents. Barns make for great breeding grounds, complete with the rodent equivalent of gourmet meals. To keep the pest problem in check there's nothing like a few cats. Farms are places for working animals – and barn cats know they have a job to do.

THE OTHER SIDE OF THE COIN

Sadly farm cats don't always receive the type of individualized care and medical attention received by some of their pampered suburban and urban pet counterparts. Often farm cats are left to breed with no thought of population control. To this day in some areas of the world numbers are kept down by drowning or breaking kittens' necks at birth. Sometimes little or no food is provided and the cats either live or die depending on the amount of prey they can capture. Although the freedom of living on a farm may seem appealing to city dwellers, the reality for some farm cats is fairly gruesome.

PROJECTING THE RIGHT IMAGE

This little white kitten isn't so sure what he's run into. It may even be the first time he's encountered a dog. Although he's a novice instinctively his reaction is right on target. Several curious things take place when a cat is fearful and apprehensive. Because cats are small, and they know it, when faced with the need for self-protection they use every trick possible to make themselves appear larger. They stiffen their legs to add some height. They bristle their fur to give the illusion of being heavier than they are and, last but not least, they arch their backs. By creating an inverted U shape with their backs not only will they look larger to the opposition, they will actually measure taller too.

Look closely at the kitten in the tree and you'll observe a curious phenomenon. Although he has no prey, his mouth is moving in a unique fashion. Both the jaw and the teeth are chattering in anticipation of capturing the prey. Often this chattering activity is more apparent in novice hunters or in housebound cats, frustrated by being forced to view their prey through one of our insurmountable obstacles. More experienced cats and those with better access to the hunt generally reserve this special jaw and tooth action for the kill.

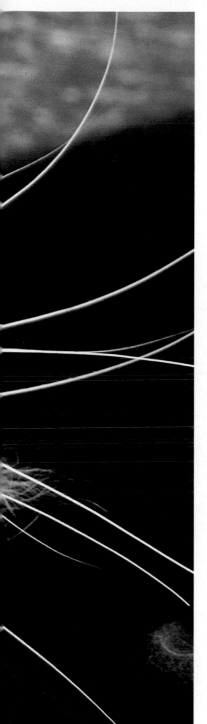

WATCH OUT!

◀ This cat's aggressive state is very apparent. The ears are pulled back flat against the head, the whiskers are bristling and the lips are raised. Before committing themselves to an aggressive or attack position, most cats will give an early-warning signal. The closer they come to the attack the more pronounced the signal will be. One example of this is the height of the raised lips. Generally speaking, the more the lips are raised and the more the teeth are exposed, the higher the level of aggression. When a cat is displaying this type of body language, respect what he is saying – and give him some space!

A REAL CAT FIGHT

▲ When cats enter into battle they use both their claws and their mouths as weapons. When one cat begins to feel he is losing, he will oftentimes roll over onto his back in a submissive position, indicating that he gives up, and the other cat is indeed the winner. Although that hasn't quite yet happened here, we can see that the standing cat may go on to win this fight because he has forced the second cat into a more vulnerable position. Often a cat fight has to do with one cat infringing on the other's territory. However, cat fights can take place at any time, even between pet cats living in the same house. If this occurs, owners should take a backseat and let the family felines figure things out for themselves as long as there's no bloodshed or injury. Any two animals living together need to work things out on their own sometimes and the more interference from outsiders, the worse the problems become.

THE SOCIABLE CAT

How sociable are cats? This is a difficult question to answer, since they are such adaptable creatures, and will make the most of whatever situation fate deals them. But, although they hunt alone, cats do appreciate company – whether human or feline. Typically, they prefer to have a choice; the Cat Who Walks by Himself may seek a friendly lap or want to play with another cat from time to time. It is usually recommended that owners keep more than one cat for this reason.

CAT COLONIES

Domestic arrangements aside, there are also colonies of feral cats all over the world. They are the result of domestic cats run wild, abandoned, or lost. These former pets breed and establish colonies in both town and country. Such colonies are estimated to have existed for centuries.

Feral cats are the only felines – apart from lions – to live in large groups. According to observers, their society seems to be based upon a matriarchy; the queen with the most kittens rules. These cats, just like your pets, establish their complicated ground rules through scent messages.

Cats' paws deposit scent, marking out different routes and transmitting information to other cats. They also rub their coats against features such as posts which they encounter along their way – another method of leaving messages for others. These messages are used to establish a kind of territorial map with private "no-go" walkways, shared highways, hunting grounds and so on. A "group scent" develops from all these individual contributions.

Clawing also leaves scented messages, and is not something a cat does just to sharpen her claws as we used to think. A number of cats may use the same piece of wood or tree trunk in communal areas of their shared territory.

Despite all these subtle rules colonies of feral cats do have fights, of course, but for the most part they appear to live as a loose unit. They sit at a distance from each other in the communal area, as if they have agreed upon the amount of space each animal can take up. This varies, depending upon the number of animals living together.

SOCIAL BEHAVIOR

We say "Hello," shake hands, or kiss each other in greeting. Cats find out all about each other through scent. By sniffing another cat's head or beneath her tail – these are both places where scent glands are concentrated – cats learn much about each other. Their body language and wide range of vocal signals expand this initial information, and enable cats to communicate in quite sophisticated ways.

As all cat watchers know, every neighborhood has its community of domestic cats. Such groups are composed of domestic as well as feral cats, and sometimes these interact: a good reason why cat

MULTI-LATERAL DISARMAMENT

Cats and dogs can coexist quite peacefully, even affectionately, in a caring household. Inevitably, there will be rivalry in this pair's relationship but her claws and superior climbing and leaping skills and his size and strength demand at the least mutual respect. Of course, she is alert to possible danger – her ears pricked forward tell us that – but we can see that the pupils of her eyes are only slightly enlarged.

BEST FRIENDS

Young animals who share their infancy have the best chance of developing a non-combative relationship. Some kittens and puppies establish affectionate ties which they maintain into adulthood. Such situations avoid the natural resentment a first pet feels at the arrival of a second who may divert the attention she has come to expect. However, it is vital in "mixed" households, whether the cat and dog grow up together or not, always to keep a check on proceedings, and stage the initial meeting very carefully. After all, over-enthusiastic friendship can hold as much danger as outright dislike.

lovers everywhere should try to control the health of feral colonies, for they can put much loved pets at risk of disease and pregnancy.

Once a group of feline neighbors is established, every member is aware of the territorial rules. They know which areas are common ground, and who lives where. There are also special pathways, the equivalent of highways, which everyone can use. Other routes are private and belong to in-dividual cats.

Most mysterious of all are the meeting areas where cats gather in groups to sit together. Nobody knows why cats do this, perhaps they are swapping gossip about the best hunting grounds. Newcomers may have a hard time until they are accepted. Unneutered queens with the largest lit-ters of kittens seem to be at the top of the ladder, whereas neutered females come much lower down the hierarchy.

Males work out who is "top cat" by trials of strength. The toughest tom fights his way to the top. From time to time younger, fitter males try to overthrow the established order by challenging the top cat. The top male dominates the largest area of land. Curiously, he is not always first

choice in the mating game. Queens on heat may deliberately choose males lower down the ladder to father their kittens.

Neutered toms, who do not have the strong male odor of an entire male, find themselves at the bottom of the heap in terms of power, but are less aggressive and territorial anyway so may not be especially humiliated by their lowly social status.

Feline territory extends throughout your house too. Parts of the house will become special to each cat, if there are several. They may choose a chair or some strange place like the top of a cupboard. When cats live together in a house they will defend it against outsiders, even though they have their own particular place within it. It is important for owners to respect these places.

BEING SOCIABLE WITH YOUR CAT

You might like to try some cat language for your-self. Some experts recommend that you get down on the floor at cat level, look into the animal's eyes, blink in a deliberate way, and lick your lips. These actions tell your cat "hello," and offer to wash her – an act of real friendship!

A FAMILY BUSINESS

There's no mistaking the relish the young ones take in their mock battles. Play is an important part of the process of socializing many young carnivores – and cats are no exception. Play fights, the earliest form of play, begin around three weeks of age with jumping, rolling and grappling. At four weeks other techniques will be incorporated as they chase and pounce upon each other. Another favorite ploy involves gripping the other with the front legs while kicking furiously with the back legs. Don't worry about the victim. Kittens soon learn too much force spoils the game.

PACK DRILL

At four weeks kittens begin to develop their hunting skills with playful sequences of pursuing, ambushing and killing techniques. Different prey demands different techniques and these have been tagged the "mouse pounce," the "bird swat" and the "fish scoop." The kittens illustrated here are playing the mouse-pounce game, the white trio apparently with some unfortunate insect. Owners frequently worry about their cats' habit of supplementing their diet with insects. Obviously there are inherent dangers in a taste for bees and wasps so it's wise to discourage it if you can. But be careful – panicking a cat at critical moments can result in exactly the fate you are trying to avoid. As for blowflies, there is a possibility they may carry worm infections but no truth in the old tale that cats who eat flies are always ill.

ROUGH AND TUMBLE

▶▼ *Cats who've grown up together often enjoy wrestling and hunting games well into adult life. Often it looks like they could kill each other in no time and when one or other gets hurt unintentionally there may be some bruised egos, but basically they are still the best of friends. If the current victim on the right really felt threatened, she'd be flattening her ears against her head.*

AFTER ME!

This country-style kitchen with its wealth of built-in scratching posts must represent nirvana for these lucky tabbies. But of course, cats being not so different from people sometimes, both of them seem to favor the same beam. Introducing a kitten to a household where there is already a cat requires sensitive handling, especially in the early stages when your first cat will need reassurance, and it is not unknown for females to settle on separate lifestyles once the younger cat reaches maturity. But ignore those who warn you off introducing a kitten into the life of an elderly cat. So long as you show your oldtimer she's as important to you as ever she was, a kitten can lighten and brighten her last years.

JOINT BENEFITS

▲ ► *One of the seals on the social bond between adult cats who have grown up together is the mutual grooming session. Called "allogrooming," its real purpose is to maintain that friendship. Still, just as it's good to have someone on hand to wield the back brush in the bathtub from time to time, having an intimate prepared to lick the places it's hard even for a cat to reach is useful. That's why you'll see a lot of attention focussed on the area behind the ears during such bouts. In the photograph above, the cat being groomed seems less than totally relaxed about it – hence the displacement lip licking. Afterwards, what could be better than a doze in the sun together? Watch a bonded pair preparing to relax together – before a fire perhaps – and you'll often see one licking the other's fur before she actually rests her head.*

THE WILD ONE

Cat meets woodchuck. Of course, in their wild state cats have learned to live alongside a variety of other animals, but judging from the erect, slightly bushed tail and raised paw the young cat isn't too familiar with this particular visitor.

THE CAT AND
THE CANARY

▶ *This isn't the first cat and canary to find true love. In the 1920s President Calvin Coolidge owned a canary, Caruso, who fell in love with Washington journalist Bascom Timmons's pet cat, Timmie. So great was the canary's attachment, the story goes, that eventually Calvin Coolidge was forced to present the besotted bird to Timmons.*

THE BETTER PART OF VALOR

◀ *Life on the farm brings a variety of social challenges for any kitten. Ducklings alone are one thing, but ducklings plus mother are* *quite another and everyone here knows it! This little creature will stay under cover until the party has passed by.*

WHAT IS IT ABOUT THESE WINGS?

Very occasionally a genuine trust seems to develop between a cat and a bird. This thrush and young cat have been brought up together, and both are relaxed in each other's company. Some experts might offer in partial explanation the theory that cats are by nature rodent hunters rather than bird catchers: a study of wild cats demonstrated that only 4 percent of them caught birds. But caution is the wiser path. Cat owners with pet birds are advised to keep them in cages on tubular metal stands designed to keep them out of a cat's reach and to place the stand where it won't be vulnerable to aerial attack!

BIG CAN BE BEAUTIFUL

Strangely, barn cats do not seem to be frightened by the size of some of their co-habitees. The larger the animal the more aware it seems to be of its size, and the calmer, more soothing, its personality is; the gentle elephant is the classic example. There are many stories of unlikely but inseparable companions – such as the race horse who refused to perform if a feline friend didn't travel to the track in the horse box too and the army mascot ram who insisted upon keeping his own furry talisman by him.

THE GOLDEN YEARS

▶ Cats are reckoned on average to become elderly in only the last tenth of their lives – much luckier than us humans, whose last third of life is accompanied by various symptoms of senile decay. One of the first telltale signs for the attentive cat owner will be when the pet begins to slow down. Her joints are stiffening up and so her jumping and climbing skills decline. Inevitably age affects social standing as an old cat finds herself less agile in defense of her territory. When this happens, make sure she is not suffering the aggressive attention of younger, more ambitious cats. The prescription for health in age doesn't differ from any other time of her life: good exercise, good diet, plenty of mental stimulation and regular checkups are still the objectives.

Stiffer joints make it harder to twist into some of the more tortuous grooming positions so elderly cats give up on the trickier bits. If your elderly pet's fur begins to look scruffy, it's a good idea to give her a hand. Old cats' habits become less flexible too, just as old people's can, and if you don't take care routine will dominate your cat's life. The stimulus of new experiences is doubly important at this stage if your cat is to get the most out of life. The changes don't have to be earth-shattering: a new food dish or perhaps a new leash can help. Introduce some new toy every two days. This needn't dent your budget. It's imaginative play you want to stimulate.

INDEX

Photographic acknowledgments
Swallow Publishing gratefully acknowledge the assistance given to them in the preparation of *The Illustrated Cat's Life* by the following organizations and individuals, and apologize to anyone they may have omitted to mention:

Animals Animals/Michael and Barbara Preed 121; Animals Animals/L. T. Rhodes 123; Animal Graphics/Solitaire 2/3, 15B, 16T, 30, 31, 58/59, 78, 93, 103, 105; Animals Unlimited 1, 13, 25, 50/51, 53, 71, 75, 83, 87B, 96/97, 110, 116/117, 122B; Ardea London Ltd 9, 38, 85T, 86, 124; Ardea London Ltd/John Daniels 46R; N. A. Callow/NHPA 102; Bruce Coleman Ltd/Jane Burton 5, 7, 14, 17, 20/21, 29, 68, 68/69, 77, 84/85; Bruce Coleman Ltd/Eric Crichton 117; Bruce Coleman Ltd/J. S. Korman 32/33; Bruce Coleman Ltd/Hans Reinhard 28, 66, 72B, 89, 96, 99, 114B, 125; Bruce Coleman Ltd/Konrad Wot 101; Stephen Dalton/NHPA 32, 49, 63, 72T, 82; Robert Estall

22, 41, 48, 78/79, 90, 107, 109, 126/127T; Marc Henrie ASC 11, 15T, 16B, 18, 67, 87T, 91, 94, 115; Mike Jackson 126/127B; London Scientific Films/Oxford Scientific Films 54, 54/55, 106/107; Anne Moretti 44; Brooke Morrison 65, 111, 112; Oxford Scientific Films/G. I. Bernard 62; Oxford Scientific Films/Deni Bown 90/91; Oxford Scientific Films/Steve Littlewood 98; Oxford Scientific Films/Avril Ramage 64; Oxford Scientific Films/P. K. Sharpe 118/119; Elaine Partington 47; Tony Stone Worldwide 23, 34; Tony Stone Worldwide/Molly Dean 22/23; Tony Stone Worldwide/Anthony Friedmann 122T; Tony Stone Worldwide/Chris Haigh 8; Tony Stone Worldwide/Chris Nowotny 81; Tony Stone Worldwide/Sue Streeter 37, 74; Jessica Strang 42, 45, 46L; Jessica Strang/Rose Gray 43; Sally Anne Thompson 18/19, 20, 24, 27, 35, 36, 56T, 56/57, 61, 73, 76, 88, 100/101, 104, 112/113, 113, 114T, 120; Sydney Thomson 38/39; Karen Tweedy-Holmes 70; R. Willbie Animal Photography 80,95; David Woodfall/NHPA 59.